Love Sutras
from the Master
Book I

Published by
Lotus Press

Love Sutras
from the Master

Book I

Vikas Malkani

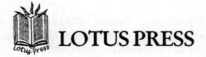

LOTUS PRESS

Lotus Press
4263/3, Ansari Road, Darya Ganj, New Delhi-2
Ph.: 30903912, 9811594448

Original Copyright © 1998 Vikas Malkani
Reprinted 3 times
Updated edition copyright
© 2004 Vikas Malkani
Revised Edition 2004
ISBN 81-901912-8-4

Published by: Lotus Press, New Delhi,
Lasertypeset by: Jain Media Graphics, Delhi
Printed at : Sharas Graphics, Delhi

Dedicated

To all believers in true love,
to all those who strive to
become perfect in it,
and to those already
merged in it.

Introduction

For long, I have wanted to write such a book—short messages, easy to understand and carry with us, and yet a comprehensive path to a higher and more complete love.

You hold in your hands the end result of that longing.

All of us are involved in relationships, in one way or another. In fact, as long as we are here in this plane of existence, we can't get away from them.

Being conscious on a deeper level that all relationships are meant to share love, we sadly start to operate and live in a totally unconscious manner while in them. We forget the real purpose for the genesis of all relationships.

To grow and become more complete, we must all make a conscious decision to move from non-love to love, from unawareness to awareness and from the unconscious to the conscious state of being, right here and now, while living within our existing relationships.

We are where we are. It is from here that we must start and rise upwards.

Open this book with faith and trust. Believe in it, it will take you higher!
All the love you seek is really yours,

Vikas Malkani

Author's Note on Updated Edition

As far back as I can remember I was always conscious of the fact that the experience of love in this plane of existence is the primary need of our inner self. An inner voice told me that our spirit takes birth only for the ultimate experience of true love. This spontaneous realization stayed with me right from my childhood years into maturity and I tried my best to learn and understand as much as I possibly could to prepare myself for the actual experience.

After my first book "Spirituality made Simple" had become a best seller I felt that time was right to share a few of my beliefs on this mystical subject with others. I put down my thoughts in simple sutras, each one designed to give a deeper understanding into the state of being called LOVE.

Since that first writing many years ago this book has touched many hearts, and I choose to believe created many true lovers.

Today, more than ever before the experience of Love is our most urgent need, and infact the only solution to our inner emptiness. I invite you to first lose yourself in these teachings, and then find yourself.

Vikas Malkani

Other Books by Vikas Malkani

1. Spirituality made Simple
2. Enlightenment made Simple
3. Secrets to Self Realization
4. To Caress the Soul Within
5. To Embrace the Heart Within
6. To Awaken the Spirit Within
7. Love Sutras from the Master: Book I and Book II
8. 'All You Wanted To Know About'
   - Stress and Anger
   - Happiness
   - Love and Relationships
   - Spirituality
   - Spiritual Healing
   - Meditation
   - Relaxation
   - Success and Self Motivation
9. The Little Treasure Book of Success
10. The Little Treasure Book of Leadership
11. The Little Treasure Book of Life

12. The Little Treasure Book of Happiness

Audio Titles by Vikas Malkani:

1. Meditation made Simple
2. Happiness.....its' Easy!
3. Secrets of Love
4. Success and Self-Motivation

In relationships, your heart can either lead your mind or follow it.

Decide which way it is to be right now!

Now, stick to your decision.

2

The secret of flowing relationships —

First, Adjustment.

Then, Contentment.

Finally, Enjoyment!

3

You must keep your relationships alive if you want to see them grow.

Death of a bond is often due to neglect.

4

Relationships are the earthly playground of God.

In them, he gives us our greatest lessons for growth.

5

Love is an emotional state of being.

It's from the heart that the stream of love flows.

Don't forget this!

At times, your mind is too logical and rational for love to flow. Thus, it pulls

you away from the very thing
you need and seek.

Become aware of this!

6

It is better to open yourself to love and risk hurt a little, than to close yourself to love and feel secure in your impenetrability.

7

None of us go into our relationships as perfect people.

We must be willing to accept this fact.

Only then can our relationships lead us to perfection.

8

We must keep changing ourselves, while being in the same relationships, and not, keep changing our relationships while being the same ourselves.

9

First learn to love one totally; only then can you grow to love all!

10

Learn to see and treat your love like water in the palm of your hand.

As long as the hand is open and your palm bent, the water stays. Close your hand to grasp the water, and you lose it. Love is just like this.

II

Love is not to be kept, possessed, hidden or rationed.

It is to be given away openly, totally, freely, in joyous abandonment!

12

Your tongue can either be a friend or an enemy to the expression of your love.

So keep a tight rein over it.

13

Every moment puts a choice before you.

No matter what your situation, circumstances or feelings, at every moment you can either act out of love or non- love.

So, choose!

14

The skill of having good relationships has to be learnt just like any other skill — slowly, step by step and with a few mistakes on the way.

In your present relationships, don't let a few small failures bring you down. Instead, use

them always to make yourself
a better giver of love.

15

If you want your relationships to succeed, be what you really are in them.

Show your true self.

Give the other person a chance to love you as you really are.

If you keep pretending to be what you are not, you are not even giving them a chance to succeed.

16

What you love is
what you give
yourself to —

Fully, totally, openly and
willingly. And in joy.

17

To him, who has loved truly, no other way is possible!

18

You cannot claim, "I love you only this much and no more." In true love, either you give fully or you haven't given at all. Either it's there or it's not.

There is no mid way in true love.

19

To love truly means to love without a selfish motive, to love for the enjoyment of loving itself.

The moment a motive is there, it's not love any more, it's a deal.

20

Love can't be forced in anyone, not even in oneself. It can, however, be kindled through love itself.

21

For you, your love is not what you will get, but what you will give.

22

As long as you fear opening yourself up completely, exposing yourself totally, you will never know what love is all about.

23

Everyday that passes without you giving love consciously, is another day wasted.

It is another day not used for its intended purpose.

24

The only thing you can really give your partner is you yourself — how and what you are, your own state of being.

If you want to become a better lover, work on your own present state of being, instead of trying to change the other person.

25

Whether your partner does their duty towards you or not, it should not stop you from doing your duty towards them.

26

To become a true lover, your joy must be sought in what you give rather than in what you get.

27

Understand this! Your every action that is not born out of love, is born out of your own fears.

28

The fastest path to the realization of the divine is that of love.

But to rise to that height, one must first learn to love all there is here.

29

On the path of love, whatever you run away from or refuse to face, you will not overcome. Even your own imperfection, fears and insecurities.

30

There is no better ground for us to learn the giving of ourselves than that of marriage, family and relationships.

31

As you enter into your relationship with another, ask yourself, "What is my greatest need here?"

A truthful answer will make things a lot smoother for both partners involved.

32

Do you give your love only if your desires and needs are met by your mate or only if they do things your way??

Then, are you giving love to your mate or to your ego??

33

In relationships, just as beginnings are natural, at times, so are endings. Don't fear endings, but at the same time, don't rush into them.

Listen to your inner voice before reaching a decision.

34

Understand that you can't force your partner to have trust and faith in you.

This will only happen when it rises spontaneously from inside your partner, based on what you say and do or don't say and don't do.

35

Learn to be happy with whatever your partner gives you of themselves.

What they give you willing and freely is yours. What they give you under any kind of pressure, is never yours.

36

It is when a relationship is going through a bad period that you find out how good the partners are.

37

Do you generally force what you think is right upon your partner??

Would you like it if they started to do the same??

38

You can see the value of your relationship with each other by honestly admitting who or what else you would place or value above each other.

39

Love gives you freedom and thus gives you stability.

Any kind of restriction to force stability is not love's work.

40

Decide what you want to have in your marriage — just togetherness or real intimacy??

Realize that there is a vast difference between the two. Once you decide what you

want, work consciously
towards it.

41

Learn to become each other's, but, beware of becoming each other's possessions.

42

How should you love??
With all your senses,
With all your abilities,
With all of your heart, mind
and body,
Totally, fully, freely,
and joyfully!

43

When was the last time you looked into your partner's eyes and said, "I love you"??

If it was more than half a day ago, it is time to say it again now.

44

Love can only be given; it can never be demanded or received by force.

Paradoxically, it is when we give our love freely, that we find it coming our way too.

45

Love's purpose is completion and fulfillment.

Love reaches there by the touching of two hearts and the merging of two souls.

46

Never forget the power of your touch to give comfort to your mate.

Hug, Hold, and Caress each other often.

47

For a successful marriage, keep a watch over the words you speak and the tone you speak them in.

Remember that your words can either heal or harm. And the choice is yours to make.

48

Is your behavior towards your partner only a reaction to what they do to you?

Or is it a conscious action as it should be??

49

Out of all of life's gifts, the greatest is that of love.

50

Within a marriage,
there is no place
for a competition between a
man and a woman.

There is only place and need
for completion.

51

Listening with full attention to your partner is one of the most important skills you need to develop. The attention you give to your partner's words should be from the mind (intellect) and the heart (emotions, intuition) both.

52

Never ever give in to the illusion that control over your partner will give happiness.

It will only give you control, and to your partner, it will give resentment.

53

You are incomplete by yourself! Accept this fact.

That's why you seek love to feel complete. This acceptance will make you grow into a more conscious lover.

54

Try replacing all of the "expecting" with "accepting" and see what changes it brings to your relationship and to your mate.

55

Distance, if it comes between a man and woman, has not come of itself or suddenly. It started slowly and small and has been allowed to grow by both the partners.

56

Admitting your fears, faults, mistakes and shortcomings to your mate in your relationship will tend to bring you closer.

It will also increase trust between the two of you.

57

Real love means that you can accept your partner's good and bad at the same time.

If at all improvement is to be created, it should be brought about with large doses of love and gentleness.

58

In real love, the happiness that you give to the other makes you happier than what you are getting.

Giving starts to make you feel complete.

59

The process of loving is not a process of possessing.

It is, in fact, a process of dispossessing.

Contemplate on this!

60

The love of your past is gone.

The love of your future is yet to come.

The love of this moment is what you have, right now in your hands.

Cherish it,

Value it,

Experience it!

61

You have a limited amount of time in any relationship. But you do have an unlimited supply of love to give within this time period. So, give as much as you can, in all ways you possibly can, while you still can.

62

To heal your partner's wounds, fears and pains, touch them with love, compassion, patience, truth and honesty.

63

The soil in the garden of your heart will grow the seeds you plant there.

Be careful that you plant the seeds of trust and not those of fear, those of love and not those of resentment.

64

One can never judge what is good or bad in a relationship, for even the loss or betrayal of a loved one can at times bring growth and awakening to the other.

65

All our scriptures tell us of the ancient and eternal law that "Anger will never cease by more anger, hatred by more hatred. Only by love can hate and anger be healed!"

— Do we remember this consciously in our relationships?

More importantly, do we practice it??

66

Never ever forget that the past never dictates the future until and unless you allow it to.

This is true in your relationships also.

67

In your relationships, forgiveness is something you must share over and over again.

It's absolutely essential.

Keep letting go to go forward.

68

God answers all questions in one way only.

— With love.

69

As you go through your life and it's many relationships, do not carry the "yesterday" into the "today" and the "today" into the "tomorrow".

Just be wherever you are in the moment.

70

Forgiveness is first and foremost for your own sake, not for your partner's.

You forgive so that you may no longer carry the load of resentment with you.

71

Deep down, at the most pure and innocent part of your being, you want to be understood, appreciated and loved.

So does your mate.

72

The circle of all life and actions operates within your relationships also. What you give out is generally what comes back to you.

73

Forgiving each other in your relationships, for all the hurts and pains caused and for all the anger and resentment felt, is one of the greatest gifts you can give to yourself.

74

If you want your relationships to work, work on your relationships.

75

If you have love, even a little of the rest can be enough.

Without love, even all of the rest will not be enough!

76

You must first believe you can create, achieve and deserve a thriving marriage.

Then, start about making it your reality.

77

Sure, your partner has both good and bad qualities in them. That's not the question.

The question is "Which ones are you always watching?"

78

Are you thankful for being in your relationship, in your marriage?

Are you carrying an attitude of gratitude for being given your partner? If not, it's time to start working on change.

79

You and your partner are both changing and growing on a daily basis. Make it a point to stay in touch with each other day to day.

80

Intimacy is being close in both your pleasures and your pains.

Love is when you seek not only the pleasures but also welcome the pains, to be able to express your love while in them.

81

In your marriage, do you give your partner the freedom to make mistakes?

If not, then why not?

You allow this freedom to those distant from you, why not also to those close to you?

82

When, and if, problems do arise in your relationship, remember that sometimes the best and most balanced decisions are made in a detached and witnessing manner.

83

In your relationships, as in your life, it is your actions of today that create the future of tomorrow. Be aware of this and learn to act consciously.

84

Love gives freedom, it does not bind or restrict. It is definitely not a control game.

Give the one you love freedom, for if you try to possess, love will never be possible.

85

If you want a plant to grow, you have to water it regularly. You have to nourish it and protect it. As it grows it becomes stronger.

Your love is just like this tree. In it's growing years, make sure you give it plenty

of care, nourishment and
protection.

86

What is your main purpose of being in a relationship like marriage? Is it not to give love, receive love and experience love?

So if you are withholding or rationing your love, for whatever reason, every step

for you will become a
struggle.

87

Even while conveying a harsh truth or reality to your mate, try and do it in the most loving way and with the gentlest words possible.

A bitter pill is swallowed easier when coated with sugar.

88

The secret of happy and successful relationship lies in this quote.

"We are each of us angels with only one wing. And we can only fly embracing each other."

— Luciano De Crescenzo.

Study it well

and remember it always.

89

Specially in your relationships, a moment of patience upheld during a wave of anger will help you to avoid a thousand moments of agony and regret.

90

Love in a marriage does not come about by itself if it does not come about in the partners first.

A marriage by itself is empty till the two partners put into it what they have inside themselves.

91

Never underestimate your partner or yourself.

Be aware that no matter how bad things may become in your marriage, at every moment you have the power to take what is wrong and make it right again.

92

One of the secrets of a happy. marriage is knowing not only what to look at, but also what to overlook.

93

A marriage start on its road to destruction the day the partners start putting other people or things before each other.

94

The path to a happy marriage and family life is through your heart and not through your mind.

— Which one do you walk?

95

 marriage prayer

O'God, help us to remember how the love between us grew. Help us to remember what drew us to each other. Help us to make that love strong and apparent and to trust and care for each other above all else so that nothing can divide or distance us. Give us the heart to speak loving and caring words and the strength to forgive and to ask for forgiveness. O'God in our marriage, make us selfless and understanding so that we can give our partner the love they need.

96

Here's a test to see how close you are to each other —

Can you disagree agreeably??

97

Love needs expressing. It must be shared between those who love. Without giving or sharing, it has no value.

So show, express, give and voice your love every chance you get.

98

If you really love your partner, all of your mental, physical and emotional faculties become absorbed in him or her.

Your partner, in a way, becomes the centre of your life.

99

Our greatest lack, and therefore our greatest need is not that of money, power, food or any external possession.

It is that of love and appreciation.

100

As we grow in our relationships, we learn to become better givers of love.

We do this by making mistakes in our loving, learning from these mistakes and thereby growing to become better lovers.

101

The walls around you that stop love from coming in have been built by you alone. And only you have the power to break them down.

Afterword

This small guide is written from my heart about a subject close to my heart and meant to touch your heart.

Please write to me if it has accomplished its purpose. I shall try and include your letters in my future work.

Vikas Malkani
www.vikasmalkani.com
vm@vikasmalkani.com

About the Author

Vikas Malkani is an internationally renowned spiritual teacher and a best selling author. He is the founder of SoulCentre and travels all over the world teaching people the ancient wisdom of the spiritual masters. He has been fortunate enough to have met and studied under various spiritual teachers.

About SoulCentre

SoulCentre conducts transformational programs worldwide for corporations, adults and children on Spirituality, Self-Awareness, Success, Leadership and Relationships.

For a complete list of our products, or for conducting SoulCentre programs in your city/country, contact us at:

www.vikasmalkani.com

vm@vikasmalkani.com